Hymns From the Third Coast

Poems by

Heather Ann Shepard

Cover design by Shay Culligan
Cover image by Barnabas Piper on Unsplash
Author photo by Heather Ann Shephard

ISBN: 979-8-90146-808-1
Library of Congress Control Number: 2026933351

Kelsay Books
502 South 1040 East, A-119
American Fork, Utah 84003
Kelsaybooks.com

Hymns From the Third Coast

For my family:
Marcus, Audrey, and Adam

Acknowledgments

Thanks to the following publications in which versions of these poems appeared:

Bronze Bird Review: “Running Under a Total Eclipse”

Crisis Chronicles Online Library: “Ode to Bats”

Girls With Insurance: “Brady Street”

The Medulla Review: “Three Graces,” “Loss of Silence”

Orange Room Review: “Sewing Lessons”

Pennsylvania English: “Betty’s Garden”

The Plum Creek Review: “Seven Blackbirds,” “Early Morning Moon” from “A Crown of Autumnal Haiku”

Rising in Hope: A tinfoildresses Anthology: “Morning Song for the Long Married”

Tiny Moments Vol IV: “Pretending a Lake Is an Ocean,” “Closer to the Stars”

Up the Staircase: “Against the Midnight”

Contents

Dancing Inside Tornadoes

I am from the Midwest and know
what tornado sirens sound like.

Walking the Ukrainian district in Chicago,
I see abandoned stores with icons left inside windows
and wonder if God knows they are still waiting for Him
to come back and buy what he put on hold.

I don’t understand the Cyrillic,
but see the foreclosure signs.

A lady who sells me matryoshkas,
says the taxes have doubled for small shops
How long can we dance inside with
this wind, lawn furniture, pieces of roof
until everyone is thrown outside?

I have pasted my jobs together,
and held them up to the sun to dry,
but my grip isn’t strong enough
to keep them from flying under a bus.

Brady Street

For Amylia

We walk together
And my patchouli has worn off.

The pubs, overfilled, spill onto Brady Street
We stop because you find an abandoned piece of art—
You are always rescuing things that need their words
Peaced together to make sense.

We speak of old loves and the time you went shopping
In the Taipei marketplace

I ask you if it is frightening to fly
And you tell me in midair, I need to let go
Like Karen Blixen when she flew over the Ngong Hills
When Denys and she saw the world like God does.

And I think
You have put on the patchwork of the whole world,
You understand the greens and terracotta squares we fly over

And this is more than two women walking down a street—
These are two souls that have journeyed
Through several reincarnations together

How else would you have known my fears before I spoke of them?

Running Under a Total Eclipse

The ghosts chase me so I run
Into crescent shadows
I am a half moon . . .
An eclipse, eclipsed
And the voices of trees aren't really trees
They are wind that cannot make up its mind

So, in which direction should I run?

When I run
The ghosts leave me becoming shadows
And I run under trees into forests
Does that mean I am hiding from ghosts?
In a moment it is night and the stars are out
Looking for me
Or am I hiding from them?
Is this narcissistic?
I am chasing ghosts

So I run, shedding shadows . . .

1990

It is dark in January when the only light overhead is not the moon, but a blue streetlamp glaring and your whiskey holding hands are not his that took my picture in the snow . . . his hands repairing everything broken in me . . . that Thanksgiving, I took him home and remembered the songs we sang at Vespers on Fridays and he dreamed in orchid's long lines of white and purple that went down my spine when we kissed in the shadow of my childhood basement. I tried on voices to see what I really sounded like—a bit of Whitter Bynner, some Sara Teasdale or the Amy Lowell poem I repeated to myself at sixteen, boned and stayed . . . saying goodbye to the girl who saw the Holy Spirit in spiders on the wall and at the piano in the chapel teaching me that voices are not heard, but felt, stabbed, plunged, expunged from experiences . . . and we smell the freshness of the wound, its gleaming pink and scarlet staring back, questioning who did you think you were? You were just like any other girl.

Ode to High Fidelity

I.

Rain pouring on the porch—
background to the timing
my parents keep,
shuffling to Dave Brubeck
on the record player.
The evening is gold
pouring in through the shutters,
light making me rub my eyes because it is 7:30
At three-years-old, humming jazz means
it is time for me to take a bath,
dress in a cotton nightgown and go to sleep
with the light of the hallway coming through
the crack at the bottom of my bedroom door.
This humming becomes the outside of
my screened window—
the sound of cicadas and cars
a block away from Wilson Avenue.

II.

Standing in front of Merrill Street's record shop
with Kim, I hold a clove cigarette,
popping vinyl leaks through the door—

Summer taught us
how far to go with a boy,
with Bowie on in the background,
and still be considered good . . .
how to buy a pack of cigarettes without getting carded.

I knew the Lord's prayer by heart,
reciting it every week in the Abbey.
But, something cracked inside me
and I wanted to listen to something new,
I wanted to tie-dye my life
with the colors of Zeppelin
to smoke in my room with the window open,
exhales drifting into the neighbor's backyard.

III.

Younge Street crashed against us, the honeymooners,
on our way to the restaurant the bellman suggested,
off an unknown street in Toronto.
As we walk, I feel the approaching music
pass over my skin,
When we walk inside
the violinist covers us
with songs gypsies sing—-
I want to stay and learn the songs
I have never heard before
because I am 24
this is what it is like
to live in another country,
be a part of another place.
I am learning new music . . .

IV.

We caught the 11:00 bus to Edinburgh
after everyone retired for the night
and took the old stone steps
to an underground pub and heard the rock music
ricochet against the old walls.

But I couldn't make peace with it in my soul . . .
because there should have been Mahler's Fifth
wandering around behind us as we walked away,
hiding behind the entryways of restaurants
when we looked back to see if it was following us
It shouldn't be something we completely heard,
it should have drifted up through the trees
with the rest of the night . . .
when we kissed in the middle of the street.

Elegy for a Lost Notebook

When you found me
I had been wandering
around in my torn dress
with twenty dollars
wadded up in my fist.

You said, is it the fear that makes you love?

and I was mute—
sixteen on an Atlantic beach
with pills in my throat
and a notebook in the sand

and a boy took my poems and read them

he said I want you to be alive . . .

So I walked, looking for God's voice in the gales

and the music played
but the stars stayed in their corners
and would not pick a partner.

Plath said everything is raw material—

the whole world tilted in worship
to the vernal equinox.

I knew I would recognize my voice when I heard it again.

Shantih . . . Shalom . . .
let the doves fly over me!

I just want one last kiss before I go back
to the Abbey and confess my sins
to the stone wall that will absorb my tears
as my cheek lay against its coldness.

But the Abbey can't tell me a new story
even with the wind carrying echoes across Long Lake.

Ode to Bats

I wait by the cave in anticipation
Of a silver rain that swirls with colors of dark,
The reflection of a mirage where I have paused
the screen so the static has time to fill me up.

This is what it means to live inside of an iris
This is what it means to hear things that others don't believe in.
Your blackness, your life of fifty years is more
than the songs you sing on a frequency that channels the universe.
I believe that you know where stars go when they die
and you know the power with which they are conceived.

By this cave, I will wait as long as it takes
To see you come out and serenade Andromeda
With your whirring that moves the air I breathe

True North

I push back tornados.
words and music
have composed me.

And the pen pierces into the eye of the storm
and gravity divides my body into sections:
above the heart
below the heart

where does my blood go
now that I have lost my compass?

There is no true North
only the memory of your face
before I went blind.

What Prayer Looks Like

Blue is the color of ink my students put on the page when they write about their loved ones wandering the streets in another dimension, veins filled with opiates . . . and I want to take a suitcase and pack their words with my jeans and journal and fly with them over the Arctic Sea. Is that high enough to reach the holy spirit? Their pain has bruises in the shape of a savior's hands—holes that make them whole . . . they teach me what love looks like after it has been wrung out and evaporates out the window but comes back in the breeze that holds up butterflies in May . . . voile movement toward the light.

Elegy for Roses

Rose and clove
Petals and calico
Sometimes I pray to you now
through a jali screen
I want to know:
Are God's eyes the color of a thunderstorm?
Does it rain in heaven?
Three weeks ago I sat under an oak tree with my harp and
    lost my voice.
Now the birds sing in my place

Seven Blackbirds

In a moment of utter despair
I looked out my window
And the universe gave me a gift.
Seven blackbirds gathered on a snow covered
Cherry blossom tree
For a moment death's voice was quieted
And there was light
To be present is like a prayer
Wind lifting worry's wings
Until it disappears
Landing in a tree, unseen.

Pretending a Lake Is an Ocean

This is your heaven my dear friend—
God's hands holding the white silk moon
in the velvet sky and the ocean singing.

You go down the cliffs and wait
for a response to your prayers—not waiting to hear words
but pictures . . . to you He has always
spoken in the haikus you see
on your evening walks

And you know that as the moon changes its shape,
your life will also . . .

Sometimes full and seamless,
sometimes crescent with sharp edges
sometimes utter light in one half and total darkness in the other.
Even though we are apart,
I see you standing at the edge
your hands lifted in the night
holding up emptiness
where the moon used to be.

Seeing No Moccasins in a Bonfire

I remember when my family
gathered across the street
for a bonfire with our neighbors.

I watched my friend by the fire,
she smiled and laughed,
her hair growing back,
cancer gone.

Our children created a light show
playing tag with flashlights
while my daughter climbed high into the
tree in the next yard . . .
and I thought of how brave she was and is now—
scaling into darkness
like No Moccasins when she freed
her husband and led him away from
the enemy camp,
taking his eagle feather staff when he passed on.

Driving to Lapeer

As I drive to Lapeer, I see the rows of bare birches against the slate sky and the landscape changes. I remember my friend telling me about lying in a prairie and feeling the thunder coming underground . . . the moving grasses and the tears of ancestors . . . and under my breath, I say Pilamaya ye. I know when I stop I will pull out my pen and wrestle with this language. It's like Rilke wrote in his letters: A work of art is good if it has sprung from necessity.

A Crown of Autumnal Haiku

Early morning moon—
yawning with me as I count
the stars next to it.

Orange moon—
open kimono threshing
fresh sleep in silk.

Autumnal oak—
branches barren, revealing
summer's kept secrets.

Burning leaves—
my childhood returning,
permeating clothes.

Sewing Lessons

I belong here on Saginaw Street
standing outside the women's dorm
on smoke breaks,
holding writing classes with women and newborns . . .

I like to read Sylvia Plath and Tupac poems
in the same breath.
GED essays become testimonies
and we count how many days they have been clean.
Their lives have been through the washing machine
and the rinse cycle
and they learn how to resew the garments
left on their backs.

They turn the fabric inside out and make something
completely new.

Against the Midnight

Every mother knows
When the moon is in the middle
Of the night sky and Ursa Major
Has passed over roofs
To the other side of midnight.

I know because I sleep lighter,
Listening for my son's gasping breath
Or my daughter's murmuring of a word
She can't say during the day.
I know because I wade into the fear
That surrounds their beds
Up to my knees and I grab hold of it
Wrestling against the midnight,
The indigo clouds.

To be a mother is to dissect fear
And scoop its insides out
Throwing them in the metal dish,
Classifying them, numbering them
And adding another index card
To the catalog—
To remember when they can't
So they don't have to carry it
Out into the world.

Three Graces

I slip out of your silk,
the color of Mecca at sunrise.

I want to be colorless and without texture
because there is a prison found in definition—
this heaviness gravity gives.

I want to have already faded
into the background, to take it all in
and be more than what worldly things classify me,

windblown and wandering,
because grace is more than the love on a woman's face,
it is what rests underneath when everything is taken away.

Beauty is more than the covering God sewed over our spirits,

because charm is a serpent biting at our ankles until we fall.

An August Afternoon

My daughter morphs in the sunlight
When she dives into that other world
Where girls become mermaids set free.

As she emerges from the deep,
She exclaims that she is a dolphin
Searching for a home.

Then my son brings a lonely turquoise earring
He claims is my newest gift
Along with a bottle cap and a hair clip
He has laid at my feet to dry in the sun.

And I am reminded
That treasure is found at the bottom of a community pool
As well as imaginary lands whose names I can't pronounce.

As I sit, a sparrow flies in landing on the lounge chair beside me,
Tilting its head as if it has something profound to reveal
To the August afternoon.

Betty's Garden

Sometimes wind blows leaves down our street
and my children chase them
running by Betty as she puts her garden to sleep
for the winter—
brown framed by marigolds . . .

Weeks before her husband died,
Betty and I stood among her tomatoes
and she pulled the dead leaves away
from the vines and said
Sometimes all we can do is let the person we love go where
    they need to . . .

it's like watching my koi fish
and wanting to hold their orange, black, and white frames—
instead I watch the shapes they create
as they huddle together in the corner of the pond.

When Betty brought Bob home from the hospital
during their last spring,
she held on to him as he walked to the door
and she opened it, helping him inside
Our hands help birth color from Earth and hold others as they
    fall away
into the wind.

Closer to the Stars

I heard that Joan Baez built a treehouse
inside of a two-hundred-year-old oak tree in her backyard
and it reminds me of how my daughter
said she wants to live in one someday . . .

It makes me happy because
there is an example of someone in this world
who is still willing to rock the cradle inside themselves
and keep the cobwebs away.

So, I will tell her to keep climbing as high as she can
and to make blueprints for a house
that is a little bit closer to the stars than the rest.

Reading a Minor Poet at 4 AM

My mentor said I should read Sara Teasdale
so I have pulled her poems out and they are
warm and astonishing, interrupting my husband's cough
as he turns over, facing our bedroom window.

The harvest moon shines a spotlight on the floor
and I wonder
when poets read the poems of others,
do they receive stream of consciousness or
an IV bag of red or clear,
always coming out differently.

I thought if I read enough, I could say something
about my son as he watched the Galilean moons
surrounding Jupiter
but the only thing I could remember was the shape of his mouth
as he looked up and said Mom, you've gotta see this.

A Pair of Swallows

It is said that swallows mate for life
and their very presence creates
a happy marriage.
Chinese leave their windows open
so that, during spring, birds can return to their nests,
inside the home's rafters.

Darling, if we left our window open,
I wonder if birds would make their home here
among us, too . . .
How many seasons would they come and go?

Would we still be here when they arrived,
or would we have moved on
even though it was still their home?
They patch their nest with fresh spring mud from the fields—
they renew what is broken.

The Storyteller

Two goldfinches,
darkened by winter,
rest on the feeder
Sharing seeds,
one shields the other with his body,
protecting her from the wind,
as friends do

The snow is gray,
the sky is gray,
the trees are brown and naked
except for three blue spruces
filled with families and songs and stories
I try to decipher for my children.

After all, what is an imagination for?

Walking on Water, Christmas Eve

Christmas Eve
I stepped onto a frozen lake
for the first time
and underneath, I saw my daughter letting go
of an ornament on our tree and how it spun—
its bleeding movement of color
showing the lines, the direction of an axis
turning away
bringing the snow, the season.

I ran, pulling her sled behind me
breathing cold,
waking a child
who couldn't understand the full circle we live in:

Truth writes she is at the beginning of its shape
and I am nearing the end
I see the tiny pencil marks that have been erased and redone
to make a perfect eternity.

I know the paper is not clean underneath
and the air I run into is burning my uncovered lungs.
How do I find the small holes in my life and patch them
to prolong the things that shelter me from what I don't want
    to believe?

Yes, with each cold breath, I am dying a little death,
passing more life into her . . .
everyday it is my joy to tear off another piece
and create pile to be left at her feet
when I walk to the end of the ice.

Clear Membrane

After Carlos Drummond de Andrade

Universe, vast universe
My heart is even more vast . . .
In between the sound of my blood moving.
My legs become long,
As if reaching ahead can change the direction of my life—
I have rewrapped it many times . . . plain and with crisp corners . . .
It is hard to wrap something when you can't see its shape.
So I stretch my arms and heart until they are so thin
They become clear membrane
And I can see all the planets and stars through them
Sparkling black splattered over all the whiteness,
All the blankness that I hear when I speak to the wind . . .
And in response it crumples up
And I navigate my way through its valleys
Clinging to my compass,
Looking for color.

Winter Beds of Snow

I wake up on New Year's Day
And look outside the window
At Betty's house, empty for the winter . . .
I like to imagine her snowy garden covered with the footprints
of angels
that only warblers and winter finches see
Because winged creatures understand one another,
songs circling the sky,
Toward All Saints Cemetery where her husband lay,
Visiting his spirit in her absence.

Office Hours

For Art Orme

We meet each week
When it is tea time in Windsor and London
And you tell me stories
About physics and Henry James
and your five children.

Thank you for helping me
Put up the world map
On the bare walls of our office,
For teaching me how to understand my son's love for cowboys
And why my students never turn papers in . . .

It will all happen in time
You say, leaning back in your chair—

Yes, life will unfold its arms
And people will come in and out of this office
And you and I will grow older each semester

Watching the snow fall outside,
Standing inside rooms and believing
In that one student that can't quite see it yet—

The truth that there is a universe in them
Waiting to sing out
The right words in the right order at the right time

Because life strings together all the mistakes, joy and failure
And hangs it in the trees to shine down on us
As we walk by.

Tea at the Zen Monastery

A two-year-old
pushes a broom
across the wood floor . . .

and his laughter rises
as a monk picks him up.

Majin brings a pot of green tea
and says

There is joy to be found in work

and he smiles at me and the child.

Everyone comes and goes from the kitchen
and the bell rings to let people in
from Mitchell Street.

There is poetry to be found
in aproned children and monks
cutting vegetables from a backyard garden
that feeds Hamtramck.

There is a song in the gate
when it is opened and then closed.

Gu Dan

At midnight
I step out
under the indigo sky
and listen to the frogs singing
together.

It was yesterday, as we studied, that Betty shared
the Chinese word for loneliness—

Gu dan.

We each leave this earth alone
and hope to find one another
among the flowers, living inside roots,
entangled, leaves shooting up
toward the sky.

The night-blooming jasmine covers
everything, entering my lungs

I sit to meditate
and a singular song remains

just quiet enough to be heard
in harmony with the air.

Morning Song for the Long Married

On this May morning,
the landscape is foggy
Yet, I can see the wood's hues deepen.

My husband plays his guitar
and two wrens sing in the tree by our window
The Earth moves even though we think we are sitting still,

We feel young even though we are older.

I remind myself that when he or I leave this world,
there will still be the remembered (words) of our conversations
entwined with the silence,
the lacing of our hands,
one soul will still follow the other around to the grocery store,
    the doctor

and the bleeding heart planted, here, to begin our perennial garden
will be there as long as one of us tends to it.

A Quilt in the Shape of Seven Seas

I opened the old package of quilt fabric meant for my sister.

Her experience is now mine.

The world is connected by seven oceans

holding together calico and snow,

sea and rocks.

How does the sea turtle know to go to the ocean after it is born in a nest of sand?

While my hands work in the purple light,

I hear the sanctuary at 5 am.

This very morning,

I exist

so I can have a conversation with the sparrow

at my window and tell her

I was made to write about the world

in every language I can understand.

Rosary

Each morning I light the candle
contemplating the Mysteries of the Lady
and my heart cracks open
light rises
roses falling into me.

This an exercise in listening,
joining my hands with the Holy Spirit
translating my selfishness to clarity
helping me hear the music
that is not carried on soundwaves

I cannot afford to travel
to Medjugorje or Lisieux
but I can stay where I am
and be ready for what comes next.

When I See Butterflies

Sometimes, I will find a butterfly
On my morning run.
It lands on the ground and flies away,
But sometimes it stays.

It's like a moment that passes when I meditate
Suspended by breath
Astonished by the fact that I am still here
And those I have lost are not

Queen Ann's Lace and Tiger Lilies look up at me,
Nourished by the creek as if to say

Don't you know why you are here?

I am not sure I know why
So I take a breath and begin again.

Awareness baptized by creek water.

Hymn From the Third Coast

I hear hymns when I cross the Mackinac Bridge
Humming beneath me in low notes

Sky meets lake
Uncertain sunset
Colors melting into the event horizon

The only way to find what I am looking for
Is to dive down deep inside
And find the answer

Hidden Frequencies

For Mr. Mo

Lake Erie has been calm
this summer—
I have said goodbyes to its sunsets

Now, I sit with my husband
our friend sleeps in the living room
watching breathing become shallow
until it disappears.

There is a vibration around and through us.
It is always there
Even though we don't hear it.

I walk over to him and
Take hold of his long fingers
And find it so strange at how still they are
Because they were always making music.

I remember conversations as song lyrics
Most of our time spent
listening for frequencies—
Irregularities hidden in the music.
his eyes, closed
smiling when recordings matched ideas

Today, we sit
discussing all the matter we cannot see,
Proven by physics
And I try to imagine what it looks like—
This is faith, isn't it?

One thing I am sure of—
When our dear friend goes somewhere else
Like the summer sunsets,
his songs will dissipate into the universe
So what is unseen, will be heard.

Writing While Running

I stopped by the koi pond
In the middle of my run
To meditate
To contemplate the contemplation
But words keep rippling toward me
Life is water
Water is life
Running into over under passing
When we run away from something,
We run toward something else
Even if we stop, the earth is still twirling

What if I let go of gravity?
I have no choice here.

Chapel Grove

This hymn is so silent
This hymn is so loud
The birds are singing on top of it
But it sounds different every time they sing
There are no prayers right now
No word for the darkest place in me
But I can sit here and wait

There is scripture in silence.

Winter Walk

I take a walk after fresh snow,

black crows leave koans to find—

My steps are the first
so someone will know I was here

I stop to watch a cardinal land
on an ice-covered Gingko tree—
Impermanence

Bloodless

I am carved out
Hollow heart
Bloodless beats
I try to walk forward
But my muscles do not cooperate.
There is a hole in the sunrise
And a shadow inside the moon
That I hide behind.

Do not leave me.

Angels at the Laundromat

5:00 AM
No one around but my angels
To hear me sing our songs

At the laundromat
I remember the first time you brought me here
And we sat and talked about how you came here
As a teenager and hang out because it was free.

Now I come here alone
Ao do our family laundry
Sometimes I loan an old friend a lighter

And I find God in the stories that people tell me as we wait
for the dryer.
I look out the window at my church across the street.
It is Holy Week now and the flowers have bloomed but my
heart is February

Then the sun rises over the trees
This is the answer You give me.
I know I will keep coming here for answers.

Kaddish in a Catholic Hospital

For my husband, Marcus

I sit with you by your hospital bed
And you discuss philosophy with air
Looking out the window
You see angels and flowers I cannot

I need to believe more

You are here with me but you leave
You go somewhere else like Billy Pilgrim

As the nights morph into days you continue to recite your poetry
as your spirit rises above your pain
Your words mean more to me because you still have a voice

The ghosts have taken some of your breath
But not all of it
Breath is smaller
Vapors of light

You were always a skeptic
You still are even now.
You are deconstructing the sounds around you

You ask me to help you mix a track we haven't written yet.

I wish we could.

About the Author

Heather Ann Shepard holds an MFA in Creative Writing and an MA in English from National University and teaches writing at Lorain County Community College in Ohio.

She has published fifteen collections of poems, including her latest, *Elephants,* from Cyberwit Press in India. *Snow and Shiuli* is forthcoming from Origami Butterfly Press.

www.ingramcontent.com/pod-product-compliance
Lightning Source LLC
LaVergne TN
LVHW090618110826
845146LV00001B/436

* 9 7 9 8 9 0 1 4 6 8 0 8 1 *